THE BIBLE ANIMAL STORYBOOK

© 1990 by Questar Publishers, Inc.

Printed in the United States of America

International Standard Book Number: 0-945564-35-X

The BIBLE ANIMAL Storybook

Written by Mack Thomas
Illustrated by Elizabeth Hagler

QUESTAR PUBLISHERS, INC.
Sisters, Oregon

CONTENTS

The New Raccoon

 WOKE UP and stretched and looked around. Everything I saw
surprised me. I didn't know where I was.
I didn't even know *WHO* I was.

I saw someone splashing in a river nearby.
He had white feathers and yellow feet
and wide wings and a big deep bill.

I ran over to talk.
"What's going on here?" I asked.
"Where am I?"

"Good morning!" he said. "Why, this is Earth. It's new.
God just made it, and He just made you!"

THEN HE splashed me.
"And God just made this water!" he laughed. "Don't you love it?"

The water was cool.

I jumped in and splashed him back.

We washed and sloshed and swished and swam in the river.

Then we climbed on a big brown rock to dry in the sun.

"God sure knows how to make a good rock," he said,
dancing around. "Don't you just love it?"

It was smooth and hard and warm to my feet.
I did some dancing too.

WE TOOK A WALK on the riverbank. "Ah, glorious!" he said.
"Don't you just love this grass and these flowers God made?"

The grass was soft, and the flowers were bright and sweet.
He picked a daisy and wore it.
I did the same.

"By the way," I said. "Who are you? And who am I?"

"We don't have names yet," he replied.
"But we can call each other 'Friend.' Okay, Friend?"

"Okay, Friend," I answered.

Then he flew to the branch of a tall cypress tree.
I scampered up beside him.

"Don't you love the view up here?" he said.

"Earth is *so big!*" I shouted. "I can't even see the end of it!"

"Someday," my friend said, "I'll take you out there
to all my favorite places that God just made.
I know where even bigger trees are! And waterfalls!
And three other rivers that roll on for miles!"

"You've seen ALL THAT?" I said. "You must have been here a long time!"

"Oh, I have," he told me. "Ever since yesterday."

SOMEONE ELSE came flying by,
someone who looked like my friend,
with white feathers and yellow feet
and wide wings and a big deep bill.

My friend looked up and smiled
and flapped his wings.
"That's my sweetheart," he said.
"And God sure knows how
to make a sweetheart!
She's my best friend.
Goodbye!"

He sailed up beside her, and they flew away together.

"Goodbye," I said quietly.

All by myself, I crawled down the tree. I shuffled across the grass,
sniffing a flower here and there. I lingered by the river
and rolled a stone or two down into the water.

But there was no one to play with.

Finally I lay down on the big brown rock.
I closed my eyes and took a little nap.

WHEN I WOKE UP, someone was lying beside me, asleep.

"Wow!" I blurted out.

My voice woke her, and she stared at me.

"What's going on here?" she said.
"Where am I? Who are you? *And who am I?*"

"This place is Earth," I told her. "It's new.
God just made it, and He just made *you!*"

I gave her a hug.

"We don't have names yet," I continued,
"but we can call each other 'Sweetheart.'

"AND I KNOW where God made a river we can splash in,
and grass and flowers we can walk in, and a big cypress tree we can climb
and see almost the whole Earth!"

"You DO?" she exclaimed. "You must have been here a long time!"

"Oh, yes," I told her. "Ever since this morning. Come on! Let's go play!"

So we did.

And I gave her my daisy.

And she's called me "Sweetheart" ever since.

My Brother's Story

ON THE MORNING I WAS BORN, my big brother told me, "I'm glad, I'm glad, I'm glad you're here! I have so many things to tell you!"

So he started telling me. "I'm already one year old," he said. "And *God* made us. And your little ears are cute. And the sun up there slides down at night. And I hurt my nose on a thornbush. And Abel says I'm his very first lamb, which means I'm special. And yesterday it drizzled all day. And...."

And then I saw a tall, strong boy walking toward us. "That's our shepherd," said my brother. "His name is Abel. He and I will take care of you. Someday soon we'll take you to see the high meadow — our very favorite place!"

Abel came close and gathered me in his arms. He softly stroked my woolly coat, and said, "Welcome to the world, little lamb!"

On a day soon after, Abel lifted me across his shoulders, and we marched away. My brother high-stepped along, staying close to Abel's heels.

We came to the high meadow, filled with gentle grass. Abel set me down by a quiet stream. I bent my head to drink — and then jumped back. In the water, right at our feet, I saw the same bright sky that stretched so high above us! How could that be?

"The world is full of wonders!" my brother told me. "That's what Abel always says."

So I drank the sky-water, and it tasted as clear and blue as it looked.

We skipped across the meadow and stopped here and there to bite off some grass. It tasted good and green, just like it looked.

While I chewed a mouthful, my brother looked up at the hills and whispered, "The world is also filled with dangers, Abel says. He says that from those hills the lion comes in summer, and the wolf in winter, and floods in the spring.

"And between those hills are wild, twisting canyons. Abel says they can let you in and never let you out."

LATE IN THE DAY Abel took us home.
We passed a field where another boy was working.
"Keep those animals out of here!" he yelled.

As Abel herded us away, my brother leaned close to me.
"Here's danger too!" he whispered. "That's Cain, Abel's big brother.
Abel says Cain can get awfully angry.
He said I should always keep away from him.

"And YOU should too!" my brother added, with a stern look.

THAT NIGHT as we bedded down in the sheepfold, I couldn't sleep.
I was thinking about all the world's dangers and the darkness all around us.

My brother said, "Don't be frightened, little lamb. You'll be safe!
Last summer a lion came, but Abel threw rocks, and it ran away.
And when winter came, so did the wolf, but Abel chased it off with sticks.
And when spring came, so did the floods, but Abel kept me high and dry.

"Besides, little lamb, Abel says that even if he were gone,
GOD is always here. You *must remember* that, my brother; if ever Abel and I
are not here to take care of you, God still watches over you!"

My brother nudged me with his nose. "Sometimes," he said,
"Abel sings the Song of Safety to me. It's his favorite — and mine too!
Maybe he'll sing it for us tonight."

And that's just what Abel did, as he came over and patted our heads:

*All that I have is Yours, O God,
and everything I am.
For You are able to keep me safe,
You are able to guide me,
You are able to welcome me home,
living in love beside me.
All that I have is Yours, O God,
and everything I am.*

When Abel finished singing, he said to me, "Good night, my little lamb."

He turned to my brother. "And good night to *you*, though *you*
aren't a little lamb anymore, are you? Yet I love you as much as ever.
You're what no other sheep could ever be: my very first lamb —
the firstborn of my flock." He gave my brother a long, long hug.

The next morning with Abel we marched to the meadow again.
All day we played. My brother pretended he was a lion.
I pretended I was a wolf.

We wandered all over, but Abel wouldn't let us get too close to the canyons.

When the sun began to slide down, Abel sat down with us
beside the stream. "You know," he said to my brother,
"I call you MY firstborn, but of course you don't really belong to me.
God made you, and you belong to Him.

"I've been thinking, and praying. God gave you and so much more to me;
so, to tell Him 'Thank You,' I will give you, my firstborn, back to Him."

THAT EVENING, as the first stars blazed in the sky...there on the high meadow
beside the quiet stream, Abel gave my brother to God.

And he sang,

All that I have is Yours, O God,
and everything I am.

With tears in his eyes, Abel lifted me to his shoulders and carried me home.
"I believe God likes my gift," he told me.

Suddenly, as we passed Cain's field, Cain stepped out from the darkness.
His face was angrier than I'd ever seen it.

Cain asked Abel to come with him. Abel set me down.
I watched the two brothers disappear in the darkness of the field.

That was the last time I ever saw Abel,
for that night Cain did something terribly, terribly wrong:

He killed his brother Abel.

THE NEXT MORNING I marched again to the meadow,
dropping several tears along the way.

The sun filled the meadow with golden light.

There beside the quiet stream, I stopped and listened.
While the wind tossed the gentle grass, I could hear the Song of Safety
coming down from heaven, in a voice just like Abel's.

So I sang along, loud and strong:

All that I have is Yours, O God,
and everything I am.
For You are able to keep me safe,
You are able to guide me,
You are able to welcome me home,
living in love beside me.

The Outsider Dove

HERE ONCE was a big boat called the Ark. Inside lived at least two of every kind of animal and bird. They were there because a terrifying flood covered the earth. But in the Ark these animals stayed safe, together with a man named Noah and his family.

Most of these creatures liked to spend their time in the Ark eating or sleeping or chatting with one another. But a certain bird — a young, white dove — was *very* different.

"HA HA HA! THAT CRAZY OUTSIDER!"

Each morning, this dove was the first animal to awaken. He started his day doing exercises that he called his "morning warm-ups" — jumping jacks, touch-your-toes, and wing-stretchers.

Then he had a quick breakfast (always oat bran with a little fruit.)

He spent the rest of the day flying back and forth inside the Ark as fast as he could, and for as long as he could without landing. When anyone asked why, he said he was *in training*. "I'll stay in good shape," he said, "so I can fly long and hard out in the real world. Someday we'll leave this boat, you know. We're all going outside!"

The other animals laughed at him, and called him "Outsider."

ONE DAY, after flying back and forth across the Ark for **127** times without stopping, the dove visited one of the giraffes.

"Hello, Outsider," chuckled the giraffe. "How's your *training?*"

"Actually, Mr. Giraffe," answered the dove politely, "I could use your help."

"Oh?" said the giraffe.

"Have you noticed," said the dove, "that you are the tallest animal in the Ark?"

"Why, yes," said the giraffe, smiling and stretching his neck as far as he could. "I *have* noticed."

The dove went on: "On the day we leave this boat, I want to be ready for life outside. And something I'll be doing out there is taking off from trees. Since you're more like a tree than anyone else in the Ark, I'd like to practice taking off from your head. May I?"

The giraffe lost his smile, and said, "Listen to me, Outsider Dove. All this *training* business — don't you know it's utter nonsense? We're *never* going outside! There's nothing out there but a terrifying flood! We'll be on this Ark forever!"

"I don't think so," replied the dove. "Besides, it never hurts to stay in shape. So will you let me practice taking off from your head?"

"If I did," said the giraffe, "the other animals would see us, and they might laugh at me. I hate to stick my neck out like this."

"*Please!*" said the dove.

"Oh, all right," agreed the giraffe. "But do it quietly. Don't make a scene."

Beginning that day, the dove added tree-takeoff exercises to his daily routine.

ONE DAY, after flying back and forth across the Ark for *198* times without stopping, and after doing *16* tree-takeoff exercises from the giraffe's head, the dove visited one of the elephants.

"Good morning, Outsider," snickered the elephant. "How's your *training?*"

"Actually, Mr. Elephant," answered the dove politely, "I could use your help."

"Oh?" said the elephant.

"Have you noticed," said the dove, "that you're the biggest and heaviest animal in the Ark?"

"Why, yes," said the elephant, smiling and proudly shifting his weight from foot to foot. "I *have* noticed."

The dove continued: "On the day we leave this boat, I want to be ready for life outside. And something I'll be doing out there is making hard landings on the ground. Since you're more like the hard ground than anyone else in the Ark, I'd like to practice landing on your back. May I?"

The elephant lost his smile, and said, "Let me tell you something, Outsider Dove. These exercises you're doing, all this flying here and there — don't you know it's utter silliness? We're *never* going outside! There's nothing out there but a terrifying flood! We'll be on this Ark forever!"

"I don't agree with you," replied the dove. "Besides, it never hurts to stay in shape. So will you let me practice landing on your back?"

"Tsk, tsk," said the elephant, shaking his head. "I can't be weighed down by your foolish concerns. Besides, the other animals might see us and laugh at me."

"*Please!*" said the dove.

"Oh, all right," said the elephant. "But do it gently. Don't make a scene."

And the dove that day added hard-landing exercises to his daily routine.

ONE DAY, after flying back and forth across the Ark for 256 times without stopping, and after doing 35 tree-takeoff exercises from the giraffe's head, and after doing 21 hard-landing exercises on the elephant's back, the dove visited one of the lions.

"Greetings, Outsider," snorted the lion. "How's your *training?*"

"Actually, Mr. Lion," answered the dove politely, "I could use your help."

"Oh?" said the lion.

"Have you noticed," said the dove, "that you have the loudest roar of any animal in the Ark?"

"Why, yes," said the lion. And he let out a roar so loud it rolled the dove over eight times and blew out a few of his feathers. "I *have* noticed," the lion said with a smile.

"Well," continued the dove as he got up and smoothed his ruffled wings, "On the day we leave this boat, I want to be ready for life on the outside. Something I'll be doing out there is flying through thunder-and-wind storms. Since your roar is more like a thunder-and-wind storm than anything else in the Ark, I'd like to practice flying in and out of your mouth while you roar. May I?"

The lion lost his smile, and said, "Give me your attention, Outsider Dove. This 'life on the outside' you speak of — don't you know it's utter foolishness? We're *never* going outside! There's nothing out there but a terrifying flood! We'll be on this Ark forever!"

"I can't believe that," replied the dove. "Besides, it never hurts to stay in shape. So will you let me practice flying into your roar?"

The lion grumbled a little and said, "I think it's a beastly waste of time. Besides, the other animals would see us doing it and laugh at me."

"*Please!*" said the dove.

"Oh, all right," said the lion. "But do it quickly and don't make a scene."

So that day the dove added storm-flying exercises to his daily routine.

ONE MORNING, after flying back and forth across the Ark for **411** times without stopping, and after doing **62** tree-takeoff exercises from the giraffe's head, and after doing an even **50** hard-landing exercises on the elephant's back, and after doing **1** storm-flying exercise in and out of the lion's mouth (he didn't like doing too many of these, for it tended to blow off his feathers), the dove received a visit from Noah himself. Noah amazed the other animals by taking the dove to a high open window, tossing him outside, and watching him fly away.

Late that afternoon, however, the dove came back. He was so utterly tired that he landed in Noah's hands with a *plop!*

And the giraffe said, "I'll bet it's still wet outside."

And the elephant said, "I'll bet there's no dry land."

And the lion said, "Maybe that dove has finally learned there's *nothing* out there for us."

But the next day the dove was awake before anyone else, doing his morning warm-ups again. After a breakfast of oat bran and a little fruit, he flew back and forth across the Ark for **516** times without stopping.

Then he did **74** tree-takeoffs from the giraffe's head.

Then he did **59** hard-landing exercises on the elephant's back.

Then he did **2** storm-flying exercises in and out of the lion's mouth, without losing a single feather.

Just a week later, Noah once more sent the dove out the window.

THE DOVE RETURNED again late that afternoon. This time he held in his beak a freshly picked leaf from an olive tree. Noah told the dove he could keep it.

The next morning, after his warm-ups and his breakfast and **554** flights across the Ark without stopping, the dove flew to the giraffe for tree-takeoffs.

"What's that in your beak?" the giraffe inquired.

"Oh, just a freshly picked olive leaf," answered the dove.

"Where did you get it?" snapped the giraffe.

"From an olive tree," said the dove.

The giraffe held his lips tight. But later, as the dove started springing up for his eighty-ninth takeoff that morning, the giraffe could keep silent no longer.

"Stop!" he said. "The flood's over, isn't it? There's land out there, and trees and grass and flowers! It's all there waiting for us, isn't it? *Isn't it?*"

"Why, yes, Mr. Giraffe, you're right."

"I thought so," said the giraffe. "Now listen to me: I'm the tallest animal on this Ark, and therefore I fully expect to be the first to go off it!"

"Just a moment!" said the elephant, coming closer. "I heard that! And let me tell you: *I* am the biggest and heaviest animal on this Ark, so I have every intention of being the first to leave!"

That very second there was an ear-splitting roar. And the lion said, "Give me your attention! I overheard your discussion, and as the animal with the loudest roar on this Ark, I have no doubt that I shall be the first to disembark!" And he roared again.

While these three argued, the dove floated upward to do flying exercises far overhead.

He did **149** circles,

and **162** figure-eights,

and exactly a dozen double-roll dives with full twists.

NOT LONG AFTERWARD, Noah sent the dove out the window again.
This time he didn't come back but instead made himself
a new home outside.

Meanwhile, the giraffe and the elephant and the lion
had to wait **86** more days to leave the Ark.

And they did *training* exercises
every single day.

Not Enough Room!

*T USED TO BE that all the camels and sheep and goats
and cattle and donkeys who belonged to a young man named Lot
lived very much together with all the camels and sheep and goats
and cattle and donkeys who belonged to his uncle, a good man named Abraham.*

And this is what happened:

Every night it was fight! fight! fight!
No one could sleep, try as he might.
Each camel was calling the other a fool.
The sheep were tearing at each other's wool.
The goats were nothing but push and pull.
It was cow against cow and bull against bull.
The donkeys were kicking
and stomping and sticking
their noses in each other's ear.
Then everyone let out a shout (loud and clear):
    "There just isn't ROOM for all of us here!

"There's not enough room to work or play;
there's not enough room to eat our hay;
there's not enough room to stretch or stroll
or run and chase or romp and roll!
We're scrunched, we're squeezed,
and no one is pleased
with the cumbersome crowdedness here;
we're crammed in the front, we're jammed in the rear,
and WORSE is yet to come, we fear!"

THEN ABRAHAM'S CAMELS had a thought
(and where it came from, likely as not,
was Old Abe himself, who was there on the spot)
and they said to the camels belonging to Lot,

"Just take the land that Lot likes best,
and we'll all move away.
God will see that we are blessed
wherever it is we stay."

The same was said by Abraham's sheep
and his goats and donkeys and cattle.
They said, "This land is yours to keep,
so we will now skedaddle!

"We'll leave this good land,

to follow the good man

named Abraham."

So all Abe's animals wandered away,
to find another place to stay…

NEVERTHELESS,
they weren't depressed.

For that very night—

for the very first night
since longer ago than you could have guessed—

they got good rest!

The Always-Thirsty Camel

AS YOU KNOW, most camels don't often get thirsty —
at least the other nine who shared a stable with me didn't.
But I was *always* thirsty. I could never get quite enough water.

One evening our keeper came to our stable and fed us
a larger-than-usual dinner. After he left, the head camel in our stable —
we called him Captain Camel — lifted his head high above the rest of us.
And he said, "Sleep well tonight, comfortable camels; our keeper told *me*
that we're all going on a trip tomorrow."

"I hope it's to the lake!" I said.

"Nope," he shook his head. "This journey will take many days.
Our keeper told *me* that we're going far away to old Abraham's old country —
the far north side of Mesopotamia. Abraham wants us to find a girl there —
the right girl to marry his son, Isaac."

"I hope I get to carry Isaac!" I added quickly. I knew Isaac was a kind man,
just like his father Abraham. On a long trip, Isaac would let me
stop and drink whenever I wanted.

But the captain huffed, and said, "Our keeper told *me*
that Isaac isn't going. Besides, you'll have plenty to carry
without him. So let's get some rest. Good night!"

"But Captain Camel," I said, "shouldn't Isaac
come along to help us find the right girl?
He's a good hunter, you know!"

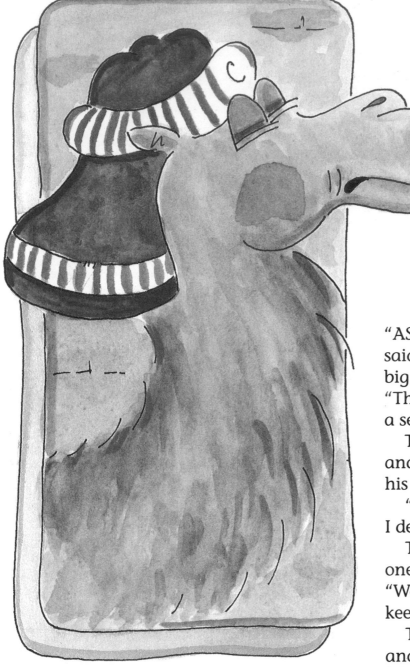

"AS A MATTER OF FACT,"
said Captain Camel with his
big nose even higher in the air,
"The keeper himself told *me*
a secret about that."

Then he closed his eyes,
and he pressed together
his big, brown camel lips.

"Aren't you going to tell me?"
I demanded.

The captain slowly opened
one eye, and he whispered:
"Well, curious camel, if you *can*
keep a secret, I'll tell you."

Then he narrowed his eye,
and said:
"Our master Abraham says
that *God Himself* will show us the right girl to marry Isaac."

"How?" I asked.

"How should *I* know?" the captain snorted. "Our keeper didn't tell me that.
And if he didn't tell *me,* it isn't important. So good night!"
He quickly shut his eye again.

I put a frown on my face and said, "If I can't carry Isaac, I don't *want* to go! Besides, whoever this girl is, she may not agree to come back with us."

"Maybe, maybe not," the captain mumbled.

"Of course," I continued, "if we took Isaac along, this girl would see what a fine man he is, and she'd be *glad* to return with us!"

Now the captain popped open both eyes. "Listen, conniving camel: Isaac *isn't* going, and you *are!* So go to sleep!"

He jerked his nose higher still, and I could almost hear his eyes bang shut. But I coughed loudly and got his attention one last time.

"*YES?*" he shouted.

"Oh nothing," I said sweetly. "I'm a little thirsty, that's all."

He growled, as only a cantankerous captain camel can.

THE NEXT MORNING we began our journey.
Abraham's most important helper, Eliezer, led us in a long, single file.

Each camel was loaded down with heavy, heavy packs.
Captain Camel told us the packs were filled with silver and gold
and other precious gifts. "Our keeper told *me*," he announced,
"that once we find Isaac's bride these gifts will go to her and her family.

"So guard them well," he snapped. "Don't be careless camels!"

As the morning sun
climbed above our heads,
I told a few camel jokes
to help make the time pass.

Even the captain liked my jokes.
"You crazy camel!" he laughed.

Then we all sang old camel-trail songs,
like this one:

It's a long way to Mesopotamia;
it's a long way from home;
so far beyond the sands of Arabia,
is the land where we'll roam.

BUT AS THE SUN got higher and hotter, I got thirstier and thirstier.
Eliezer would let me stop and drink only at night,
when we camped by a stream or a well.

Each day was the same: I kept getting thirsty…

And when I got thirsty, I wished I was carrying kind Isaac
instead of those heavy bundles…

And when I thought about Isaac, I thought about
Captain Camel's secret. *Just how,* I wondered,
can God show us the right girl to be Isaac's wife?

One hot afternoon, we raised our voices in an old song called "The Sands of Time Are Slowly Sinking."

But I changed it to "The Sands of Time Are Not for Drinking" because my mouth was so parched with thirst.

I could think of nothing else but water.

WE FINALLY SAW a town ahead.
Eliezer steered us toward it,
though he seemed to be going uncommonly slow.

I whispered to the camel next to me,
*If I don't get a drink in the next two minutes,
I think I'll die!*

The captain turned on us and shouted,
"Quiet, complaining camels!
We are near our journey's end!"

JUST AHEAD OF US, right outside the town walls, we saw a big well.
I was overjoyed. But when it was only a few steps away, Eliezer stopped,
and didn't lead us any closer.

In my dry, scratchy voice I asked the captain, "What are we waiting for?"

"*SHHHH!*" he answered.

We watched as Eliezer's camel got on his knees, and Eliezer got off.
Then Eliezer also kneeled, and started praying: "O Lord, please be kind to us
and show us the girl to be Isaac's wife. Send her out to the well right now.
And when I ask her for a drink of water, I'll know she's the right girl
if she offers to water the camels also."

I thought this was a perfect prayer, so I prayed too:
O Lord, please send her out here, and send her quick....

Before Eliezer opened his eyes, a girl started walking out from the town
toward the well. She was beautiful, and she was carrying a water jar.
She must have been coming to get water for her family.

WHEN THE GIRL got nearer, Eliezer rose from his knees
and politely asked her for a drink.

"Yes sir," she said, "why of course."

She let down her jar into the well, then drew it up. It was running over
with cool, clear, sparkling, splashing, wet, wonderful water.

She handed the jar to Eliezer...and I thought I would surely die
as I watched him take a long,

                              deep,

                                          satisfying drink.

Eliezer slowly handed her back the jar. Then the young girl looked my way.
Her eyes were as clear and sparkling as the water from the well.
She kept her gaze on me for a moment, then turned again to Eliezer
with a look of concern.

Her voice was like a gentle stream. "Shall I water your camels also?"
she asked.

"WHY CERTAINLY!" I croaked. I charged ahead and knelt at her side.
I took a quick sideways glance at Eliezer, and I saw him smiling
and nodding at the girl.

She drew more water from the well with her jar, and poured it into a trough
by the well so I could drink it. She kept drawing more and more,
and I kept drinking.

I watched her while I drank, and I thought, *This girl will be the perfect wife
for Isaac; she's kind to camels, just like he is.*

When I had swallowed about ten gallons, I stepped aside
and let other camels have some. When they finished,
I drank another gallon or two, plus a few extra sips.

To thank her for the water, Eliezer gave her a gold ring and two gold bracelets.
She said her name was Rebekah, and she told him all about her family.
"We have room for you and plenty of food for the camels," she said.
"Why don't you stay with us tonight?"

SO ELIEZER stayed that night in the house with Rebekah's family and told them all about his prayer and all about Abraham and Isaac.

We camels stayed in a fine stable. We had big piles of grain to eat and big piles of straw to sleep on — and, of course, lots of water to drink.

THE VERY NEXT DAY, sure enough, Rebekah decided to go back with us and marry Isaac. When it was time for her to choose a camel to ride during the long journey ahead, Eliezer pointed to me.
"How would this one do?" he asked Rebekah.

"He's a fine-looking camel," she said with a smile.

I knelt as low as I could so she could climb on easily. Behind me I heard the captain snickering, *"Oh, what a cute, cuddly camel!"* But I paid him no attention.

And you know, the trip home seemed to go so *fast*...perhaps because Rebekah let me stop and have a drink whenever I wanted.

The Stripe, Spot, and Speckle Story

I T WAS A GOLDEN summer evening, just right for a bedtime story. Granny Nanny, the oldest goat in Father Jacob's herd, was waiting under the big old oak tree. But the little goats and sheep were fidgeting here and there, complaining about their markings:

> *"Just look, Granny Nanny, and see what we've got:*
> *Everywhere a spot or a dot or a jot!*
> *And some of us are streaked, and some have speckles;*
> *some are flecked, and some have freckles;*
> *some have blots, and some have blotches;*
> *some wear stripes or sprinkles or splotches!*
> *Everywhere a speckle or a stripe or a spot!*
> *Granny, they're ugly — the marks we've got!"*

Granny just smiled and said,

> "I know a story about just that…
> so come on over where Granny's at!"

The lambs and kids flocked around her, saying:

> *"Baaa! Baaa!   Bleat, bleat bleat!*
> *Granny tells stories that can't be beat!"*

When everyone was close and quiet, Granny said,

> "Your many markings may seem a bit odd
> until you remember: They were given by God!"

> *"How do you know?"*
> said the little goats and sheep.
> *"Tell us, Granny Nanny,*
> *before we go to sleep!"*

Granny Nanny settled down in the grass, lifted her eyes to the evening star, and began.

She told how Jacob once lived in a faraway country. "Father Jacob spent fourteen years there," she said. "He worked long and hard to care for his uncle's animals."

THEN THE LITTLE goats and lambs around Granny Nanny chanted,

"Fourteen, fourteen long, hard years—
Hard work, hard work, up to his ears!"

"That's right," said Granny. "Jacob labored very, very hard
with his uncle's sheep and goats.
"Sometimes the sun was so hot it burned his nose —
but Jacob stayed in the field with those animals.
"Sometimes the night was so cold it nearly froze his toes —
but Jacob didn't leave.
"There were times when a little lamb was sick or afraid
and needed his help —
and Jacob got almost no rest at all.
"Finally Jacob decided it was time to leave that faraway country
and go to God's Promised Land, and he had a big family to take with him.
He asked his uncle if he could also take some of those sheep and goats
that he'd watched over so well all those years.

"But Jacob's uncle didn't want him to go. And he didn't want him
to take any sheep and goats either. So Jacob said, 'Okay, Uncle;
I'll work a little longer for you. And when it's time for me to leave,
I'll take ONLY the sheep and goats that have *stripes,* or *speckles,* or *spots.'"*

Then the little ones at Granny Nanny's knee said,

"What a strange thing! We're quite perplexed.
Tell us, dear Granny, what happened next?"

"I surely will," Granny said. "That very night Jacob saw a newborn goat,
and that baby kid had spots all over it. And do you know who that baby was?"

The little ones answered,

"No, Granny Nanny — who could it be?"

"It was ME!" said Granny. "That baby was ME!

And from that time on," smiled Granny, "almost ALL the newborn goats
and all the newborn sheep on that farm had *stripes* or *speckles* or *spots!"*

Suddenly, all around Granny the little goats and lambs
jumped and danced and shouted,

"Why? Granny Nanny, why, oh why?
That's as crazy as camels that fly in the sky!
It's as funny as foxes who eat pepper pie!
So why, dear Granny? Tell us why!"

Granny Nanny wrinkled her nose and said, "Well, little meadow-munchers,
I know Jacob tried to *make* it happen, but it was *God* who really did it —
and Jacob said so himself!

"SO WHEN JACOB and his family came to the Promised Land, they brought along more striped and speckled and spotted animals than you could shake a tree-branch at. And those very animals were your grandfathers and grandmothers, your fathers and your mothers."
    So all the striped lambs and kids around Granny smiled and said,

And all the spotted lambs and baby goats said,

And all the speckled lambs and baby goats said,

Then everybody went to sleep — Granny Nanny too.

Big Balaam's Beast

I ALWAYS WANTED TO LIVE on a quiet farm and pull a plow. But I didn't belong to a farmer. My master was a magician who was always traveling to faraway cities.

His name was Balaam, and people called him "Big Balaam." He was fat. He was so heavy to carry that it built up my muscles. People said I was the strongest donkey they'd ever seen.

My master was as famous as he was fat. Everyone knew about Big Balaam, and we got a royal welcome wherever we went. People gave us their warmest words of greeting…their finest food…their softest beds.

But I was tired of it all. I wanted to work on a farm. I sang to myself,

> *Hee-haw, hee-ho, hee-hay, hee-HOW!*
> *I wish I could work behind a plow!*

Balaam's neighbor was a farmer, and he had a donkey too — *and* a plow. His donkey once told me how he wished he could travel to faraway cities, just like I did.

"It's not nearly as much fun as you think," I answered him. "I'd much rather pull a plow through soft dirt on a fine spring day, like *you* do."

ONE DAY strangers from a faraway land came to see Balaam.
They wore rich robes and had fancy turbans on their heads.
They also carried big bags of money.

"Why have you come here with all that money?" asked Balaam.

"Would you like to have it?" they said.

That's a silly question, I told myself, because I knew
Balaam's favorite thing to have was money.

"That's a silly question," said Balaam. "Of course I'd like to have it."

"Hahhh," they smiled, "then we have a job for you,
so you can *earn* this money. You're a magician, and you know how
to do terrible, horrible magic, don't you?"

"Yes," answered Balaam.

"And you know how to do say terrible, horrible things about people
that will drive them away, don't you?"

"Yes again," answered Balaam.

"Hahhh," they smiled again. "Then return with us to our country,
and say terrible, horrible things against the people of God.
These people have moved close to us. There are too many of them,
and we don't like them *or* their God. We want you to drive them away —
then we'll pay you this money."

At first Balaam said no to them. But when they came back again
and promised even MORE money, he said, "Okay; I'll come."

When Balaam climbed on my back so he could ride away
with the strangers, I said to myself,

> *Hee-haw, hee-hi, hee-hay, hee-HOO,*
> *I think we're getting in trouble, I do!*

WE PASSED our neighbor's farm, where his donkey was pulling a plow through soft dirt on that fine spring day.

That's what a good strong donkey like ME should be doing, I thought.

But I kept on going, giving Balaam a good, gentle ride, just as I always did. I told myself I should have a good attitude. I should stop thinking about wanting to be a farmer's donkey, and just accept whatever my lot in life. So I sang to myself,

Hee-haw, hee-how, hee-ha, hee-HAY,
I wonder what I'll see today?

JUST THEN an angel of the Lord appeared in front of us, standing in the middle of the road. He was waving a sword and was staring at Balaam.

"Hee-HO!" I called, and I jumped off the road.

But Balaam didn't notice the angel. The strangers didn't either. When they saw Balaam and me off the road in a field, they began to laugh.

"What's the matter, Balaam?" they joked. "Are you lost? *Ha! Ha! Ha!*"

That made Balaam angry. He gave me three whacks with his stick — hard! — and made me get back on the road.

The angel was gone.

SOON THE ROAD passed between two walls close together. There I saw the angel and his sword once again.

There was no room to get off the road. So I called out "Hee-HAY!" and pressed close to one of the walls.

That made Balaam's foot get smashed. When he screamed in pain, the other men laughed even more, and said, "Did you kick the wall, or did the wall kick you? *Ha! Ha! Ha!*"

Balaam didn't see the angel this time either. "Dumb donkey," he said. He gave me five hard whacks with his stick.

THEN THE ROAD between the walls became so narrow
that there was absolutely no room on either side of me.
Once more I saw the angel, but I couldn't get out of his way.

"Hee-HOW!" I called, and I sat down right in the road.

"Did you break your donkey's legs?" the other men called out.
"Ha! Ha! Ha!"

They laughed so loud it must have hurt Balaam's ears,
because they were turning red.

Balaam waved his fist at me, and started whacking me again.
I'm a big, strong donkey — but Balaam's beatings were beginning to hurt.
I felt like telling Balaam a thing or two.

This time the angel didn't leave. As Balaam kept whacking, the angel said,
"Go ahead, Donkey — talk to Balaam."

SO I TURNED AROUND and faced Balaam, and in his very own language I said, "Why are you beating me?"

Balaam was so surprised he dropped his stick. "I'm beating you," he answered, "because you're doing dumb things, and it makes people laugh at me! If I had a sword, I'd slay you!"

"But I'm your *very own donkey*," I said. "I always give you a smooth, gentle ride. Maybe there's a good reason for what I did to you today!"

I nodded my nose toward the angel.

At last Balaam could see him! And he saw the angel's flashing sword.

Balaam fell to the ground, shaking all over.

The angel stood over him, and said, "Balaam, it's a good thing for you that your donkey saw me, because I almost killed you. You're in danger, Balaam. You can go ahead with these strangers if you want to. But you'd better be careful what you say!"

The angel gave his sword one more flash, and disappeared.

Balaam didn't speak another word the rest of the trip.

Neither did I, except to myself. I said to myself,

> *Hee-haw, hee-ho, hee-hay, hee-HI;*
> *I hope that angel will stay nearby!*

WHEN WE GOT to the strangers' country, their king met us, wearing a shining crown, and a purple robe, and a fancy fur cloak, and a mean face. He showed Balaam a huge pile of moneybags. Balaam's eyes sparkled when he saw them.

"All this money is for you," the king said, "as well as our finest food and our softest beds. But first, I want you to drive away God's people. Come with me, and we'll climb this mountain. From the top you can see God's people far below, and you can say your terrible, horrible magic against them."

I carried Big Balaam carefully up the mountain.

AT THE TOP, we looked down at God's people. And the king said, "Now, Balaam! Let 'em have it!"

But Balaam said, "First let me think what to say."

He stepped aside, and I followed him behind a tree. There I saw the angel again. "Hee-HI!" I sounded.

Balaam saw the angel too, and bowed low. The angel sang a song, and very carefully taught it to Balaam.

"Are you sure you know it well?" said the angel.

"Y-y-y-yes, yes," answered Balaam.

"Good! Now whenever you speak about God's people," the angel warned, "always sing this kind of song. If ever you don't, this Donkey just might have more surprises for you!"

We walked back to the king, who said, "Now, Balaam! Now let 'em have it!"

"I'll speak now," Balaam told the king. "But I'll say what I *have* to say."
Then he sang the song from the angel:

> God's people will always be many;
> God's people will always be strong;
> God's people will always have God on their side,
> with blessings as big as the world is wide!
> For God loves his people—it can't be denied—
> He makes them a mighty throng!
>
> Look for their blessings — you'll find PLENTY;
> look for their curses — you won't find ANY!
> God's people are strong;
> God's people are many;
> He makes them a mighty throng!

"Well," Balaam said to the king, "that's all I have to say.
Give me my money, and I'll be on my way."

But the king was hotter than fire. He clapped his hands in Balaam's face.
"You said *GOOD* things about God's people!" he thundered.
"Balaam, you can't have my money — not a single penny!"

"But I want it!" Balaam shouted.

"NO!" the king roared, "Go home, and don't come back
until you're ready to speak *BAD* things against the people of the Lord!"

So we went home. This time Balaam walked beside me.
For some reason he said he didn't feel like riding me anymore.

THE NEXT TIME the strangers came to see Balaam, they promised him
twice as much money as before — "If you'll just ride back with us," they said,
"and help us do terrible, horrible magic against God's people."

"Okay, I'll come," Balaam said. "But first, wait here."

While they waited, Balaam took me to the neighbor's farm.
"You can have *my* donkey," Balaam told the farmer, "if you'll give me *yours.*"

"That's fine. Let's trade," said the farmer, for he could see
how strong I was.

As he walked away, Balaam leaned over and whispered in my ear:
"You only cause me trouble, dumb donkey! *I want that money —*
and neither you nor any angel can stop me now!"

Then he hustled away.

MANY WEEKS LATER we heard that Balaam and the strangers
tried to fight against God's people, but God's people won the battle,
and the evil king and Balaam were killed.

As for me, I could now spend one happy day after another in the field
with the farmer, working and singing:

Hee-haw, hee-ho, hee-hay, hee-HOW!
It's wonderful work to pull a plow!

READ
NUMBERS 22-24 31:7-8

The Lazy Ant

BESIDE AN OLD DUSTY ROAD long ago there was an anthill. In and around and all over that anthill were thousands of ants working like crazy. They were storing up food for the winter.

They had to find the food, carry it back to the anthill, pack it carefully inside, then go back and get more.

While they bustled along, they sang a working song.

> *Let's work!*
> *Don't shirk!*
> *Just work and work and work…*

Bring in the stuff —
more than enough!
Be extra tough,
ready and rough —
Huff and puff with all your spuff!
Work!
With perk!
Let's work and WORK and WORK!

"You guys have gone berserk," said one ant to all the others
one early morning, as he watched them rushing by.
"I'm not going to work anymore!" he added, as he sat down near the road.

The other ants scolded him as they passed: "Hey you — get busy!"
they said, or, "You're nothing but a lazy ant!" or,
"Get up and start huffing and puffing with all your spuff!"

But it was no use. The lazy ant didn't budge.

THAT AFTERNOON the other ants quit working long enough
to gather around the lazy ant. Their faces looked heavy and somber.
And they said to him, "We've decided
you can no longer be an ant!"

"What do you mean?" he said.

"You're a disgrace to the name *Ant*. Everybody knows ants are good workers.
But *no one* would guess that looking at *you!* If you won't *act* like an ant,
then you can't *be* an ant!"

They turned to go back to work, saying, "We're busy now, so goodbye,
you lazy whatever-you-are!"

The lazy ant didn't know what to do.
So he stomped out into the middle of the road.

He turned back once, and shouted to the others:
"What do you expect me to *be?*
A hippopotamus?
Or a whale?
Or an eleph-ant?"

But no one took notice of him.
So he turned and just kept marching down the road.

HE HAD TAKEN only a few steps with each of his six legs,
when suddenly something blocked the sun above him. He looked up —
far up — and saw that he was in the shadow of a man and a child!

"Oh no!" he cried. "I'll be stepped on! I'll be crushed! I'll be killed!
I've got to get out of the way!"

He darted to the right side of the road.
Then he changed his mind and dashed to the left.
Then he changed his mind again and rushed back right.

Then he turned again and lost his sense of direction.
So he just kept running in circles.

Finally all six of his tired legs went out from under him,
and he dropped in the dust.

Looking up he saw the feet
of the man and the child,
standing still beside him.
Between the child's sandals
was a tiny breadcrumb.

Lifting his eyes higher,
the ant saw the man's purple robe.

Raising his eyes even higher, he saw two noble faces looking down.
And on the man's head was a golden crown.

"It's the KING!" the ant gasped.

He heard the king say, "Never be lazy, my son, but learn to work hard—like the ants do. In fact, let's watch *this* one for a moment." The two faces stared down at him.

So the ant got up on one leg, and then another, then another, and another, and another, and the last one too. And he raced to the breadcrumb.

WITH ALL HIS MIGHT, he lifted the crumb high above him.
It was heavy, and hard to balance. But by putting one foot
in front of the other, and then another, then another and another —
again and again and again — he carried the crumb all the way back
to the anthill (where the other ants smiled at him).

He stored it carefully inside, then turned to go back for more.

Outside he saw the king and his son proceeding down the road.
And he heard the king say, "Now *that,* my son, is a REAL ANT!
Work hard like him — and you'll be wise."

READ
PROVERBS
6:6-8 & 30:25

Solomon's Smelly Stallion

ING SOLOMON — the world's richest and wisest ruler — owned twelve thousand horses. Each one cost a hundred and fifty pieces of silver.

They were splendid-looking horses — all except one. This one horse was a gray stallion with fine muscles and legs. But he didn't *look* fine or *smell* fine, for he wouldn't let the stableboys wash him. He was dirty, dirty, dirty.

So he never got to be in a parade, or pull a chariot, or carry a prince. Nobody liked to be around him, except the horseflies.

Everyone called him the Smelly Stallion. "I don't care what you call me," he said. "I don't want to be clean."

But really, he DID want to be clean. He just wasn't ready yet.

One morning everyone in Jerusalem was talking about exciting news. The great Queen of Sheba, the world's richest queen, was coming to Jerusalem to see for herself how rich and wise King Solomon was. She was to arrive that very afternoon, and she was bringing gifts for Solomon: more jewels and pieces of gold than most people could count, and more spices and sweet perfumes than most people in Jerusalem had ever seen.

That morning everyone in Jerusalem took a bath. They wanted to look and smell their best for the Queen. The stableboys cleaned all the horses, except the Smelly Stallion. "I don't care to see the Queen," he said. "I'd rather stay dirty and smelly."
He just wasn't ready to be clean.

IN THE AFTERNOON, King Solomon came out to meet the Queen.
He had carts loaded with good food for the Queen and her servants to eat.
And he brought his finest horses to show her.

   He also brought the Smelly Stallion, though no one knew why.
The horseflies came too.

The Queen of Sheba saw the carts of food and the fine horses.
Behind King Solomon she saw his splendid royal city.

"I see you're very rich," the Queen remarked.
"I've also been told you're very wise, and I have a few questions for you."

"WHAT DOES a wise ruler do," she said, "if she catches a servant
stealing gold from the treasury?"

Solomon said, "A wise ruler ties a heavy bag of gold to the man's hands,
and make him carry it everywhere till he's SO tired he promises
never to steal again. Then the wise ruler tells him one of my proverbs:

How much better to get wisdom than gold."

The Queen smiled.

"And what does a wise ruler do," she said, "if her son is very sick and very sad?"

Solomon answered, "A wise ruler brings in clowns who can dance and prance and frolic and rollick, and who can tell that ailing boy every joke in the kingdom. For I've written another proverb that says,

A cheerful heart is good medicine."

The Queen smiled once more.

JUST THEN she caught sight of the Smelly Stallion with his halo of horseflies. *And* she began to smell him.

She wrinkled her nose. She crinkled her mouth. And she twinkled her eye. She said to Solomon, "And what, may I ask, does a wise ruler do with a horse that smells rotten and rancid and reeky and rank?"

And Solomon answered:

"When a visitor comes bringing gifts of spices and sweet perfumes, the wise ruler makes that animal carry all those fragrant gifts to the palace storehouse — one load after another — until the horse smells spicy and sweet."

AND THAT'S JUST what Solomon did.

It took the stallion half a day to carry it all, and with each load he smelled spicier and sweeter.

When he finished, he smelled SO spicy and SO sweet that it made his eyes water and his nose itch and his ears droop. NOW he was really READY to be washed.

So he let the stableboys clean him, and he liked it so much he decided from now on to let them wash him whenever they wanted.

Later, when King Solomon said goodbye to the Queen of Sheba, he quoted one more proverb:

Perfume and spices bring joy to the heart,
like the pleasure of a friend's good advice.

· READ ·
1 KINGS 10
PROVERBS 16:16, 17:22 & 27: 9

The Raven Raiders

 IGH ATOP A ROCKY CLIFF,
four birds stood in the sunlight.
They were ravens — black and shiny.

One was short.

One was skinny.

One had a red beak (because he always ate red berries.)

And one was a head taller than the others,
standing straight and noble like the leader he truly was.

"Attennnnnn-SHUN!" the Big Raven called out.

The other three birds clicked together the heels of their little bird feet,
and gave their leader the Raven Raider salute.

"MY FELLOW Raven Raiders," the Big Raven said.
"As you know, this land has been sad and sick for a long time.
People have forgotten God. They're bowing down and praying to silly statues
made of wood and stone. Even King Ahab is doing this wicked nonsense!"

"That Ahab is acting awfully foolish," said the Skinny Raven.

"Yeah," said the Red-Beaked Raven, leading the others in a chant:

Ahab, Ahab,
bowing to a silly slab,
praying only crazy gab—
Ahab, Ahab!

The Big Raven raised a wing to signal for silence.
When the others were quiet, he continued:

"None of this, of course, is hidden from Almighty God.
And God has chosen a man to challenge King Ahab's wickedness.

"That man's name is *Elijah.*

"Yesterday, on God's orders, Elijah walked up to Ahab and told him
that God will now bring judgment on this land!"

"That sounds bad," said the Red-beaked Raven. "What does it mean?"

The Big Raven clucked his tongue. "Elijah declared
that until he himself says differently, there will be *no more rain.*
This land will dry up and keep getting drier —
day after day, and year after year."

"No rain!" said the Short Raven. "That means crops won't grow in the fields!"

"And people will run out of food!" added the Red-beaked Raven.

"Yes, food will be scarce," said the Big Raven, "until Ahab and all the people
see and understand that God is the One True God!"

"I'll bet Ahab is angry at God AND Elijah!" said the Skinny Raven.
"You know how mean Ahab can be. Is Elijah safe?"

"Elijah is truly in danger," the Big Raven answered. "So God told him
to run away from Ahab, and to hide in Kerith Canyon.
He's on his way there at this very moment."

"I know that canyon," said the Red-beaked Raven.
"It's a good hiding place — well protected. And a stream runs through it,
so Elijah will have water — at least for a while.
But there's nothing there to eat. What will he do for food?"

The Big Raven clucked his tongue again. "Well, my brave bird brothers,"
he said. "Elijah isn't the only one to whom God is giving orders these days."

THE BIG RAVEN spread his wings wide. "My fellow Raven Raiders,"
he announced. "*WE* have been commanded to provide food for Elijah!"

"We could take him red berries!" suggested the Red-beaked Raven.

"No," said the Big Raven. "Elijah is God's good servant,
and he has much hard work ahead of him.
He needs *stronger* food — bread and meat!"

"But where can we find it?" said the Skinny Raven.

"I have a plan," the Big Raven answered. "Tell me, my brothers:
No matter how little food there is in the land —
in which house will there always be plenty to eat?"

The Short Raven let out a gasp.
"Do you mean — *the palace of King Ahab?*"

"Exactly," said the Big Raven.
"Our orders are to bring Elijah breakfast and dinner every day.
So twice a day we'll enter the palace kitchen,
take what bread and meat we can find,
and carry it to the canyon.
That's the plan."

Then he strutted a few steps and added,
"My brothers, *we* are the Raven Raiders — the finest flying force in all the land.
I know you'll join with me now to carry out this dangerous mission
with good courage, good sense, and good cheer."

Then he called out again, *"Attennnnnn-SHUN!"*

As they all stood straight, they sang the Raven Raiders Anthem.

118

EARLY THE NEXT MORNING, above the palace kitchen,
four black birds circled in the sky. They could smell breakfast cooking.
When it smelled good and ready, they flew down through an open window.

Inside they picked up some hot beef sausage and pancakes.
The cook let out a scream, but before he could do anything more
the Raven Raiders were back out the window.

The food was still warm when they got it to Elijah in the canyon.
He was all smiles, and said "Thank you" after almost every bite.

That evening the ravens went back to the palace. The kitchen window
they used at breakfast was closed, but they found another one.

Inside they grabbed three loaves of fresh bread and a mutton steak,
while the cook waved his hands and threw spoons at them.

"What fabulous food!" said Elijah when they brought him his dinner.
"I can't imagine where you find such a noble feast!"

THE NEXT MORNING, every window in the palace kitchen was closed.
So the Big Raven knocked on the kitchen door with his beak,
then quickly hid. The cook opened the door.
When he stepped out further to look both ways,
the Raven Raiders flew swiftly inside behind his back.

They took away several sirloin tips and some biscuits.

They tried the same thing that night.
A different cook answered the door, and the trick worked again.

SO ELIJAH had beef ribs and rolls for dinner.

"Another magnificent meal!" he said.
"You ravens sure know where to find tasty treasures!"

The Raven Raiders found lots of new ways
to get in and out of the royal kitchen —
through other doors and windows
in other parts of the palace,
and even through holes in the roof here and there.
On several mornings they arrived at the palace early
and went down the chimney before the cooking fire was lit.

"I just don't know how you do it,"
Elijah would say with a bright smile
when they brought him another meal
of roast tenderloin
or beef pot pie
or stewmeat
— and countless fresh loaves of bread.

And Elijah always gave
big bites of everything
to the ravens.

One
evening
at dinnertime,
the Raven Raiders
came near the palace,
and the Short Raven with
his searching black eyes saw
something moving behind a tree
in the kitchen courtyard.

He immediately reported it to the others: "Suspicious movement behind tree
one stone's throw in front of kitchen door," he said in a quiet, even voice.

The other birds looked down at the tree
and saw something sharp sticking out behind it. It moved again!

"Sighting confirmed," said the Big Raven.
"Possible soldier with bow and arrow. Reverse course at once.
We'll circle back and resume approach at lower altitude."

The Raiders turned quickly and flew far out of sight of the palace.
Then they turned around and headed back, but this time
they flew only inches above the ground.

The Red-beaked Raven said quietly,
"Request permission to attempt diversionary tactic."

"Like what?" said the Big Raven.

"Combing the soldier's hair," was the answer.

They all laughed. "Permission granted!" said the Big Raven.

THEY SAID NOTHING MORE as they came nearer the palace.
Quietly, quietly, quietly they flew, skimming over grass and rocks and roads.

Behind the tree they could see the soldier staring up into the sky.
He had an arrow to his bow-string, ready to shoot
at the first raven he saw above him.

SUDDENLY the Raiders flew past the man's knees.
Meanwhile the Red-beaked Raven rose to the soldier's head
and fluttered back and forth through his hair.

The soldier dropped his bow and arrow,
and swatted and sweated and shouted and shook.

Then he ran to the kitchen and burst through the door.

The birds followed him in.
They quickly selected some lamb chops for Elijah's dinner,
and flew out the open door.

"Once again," said the Short Raven as they flew away,
"Elijah will not go hungry.

ONE MORNING, after he and the ravens shared a bountiful breakfast of toast and roast beef, Elijah said, "Before you Ravens go, I must tell you something: This is our last meal together. God told me last night it's time for me to go away. He has chosen someone else to take care of me now in another place."

Then Elijah stood and pointed to the sky. "Of course," he said, "someday, when God says the time is right, I'll stop hiding, and again I will meet King Ahab, and show him that the Lord God is the One True God. Then rain will return, and the land will grow food once more.

"Perhaps in those happy days, my friends, you and I will see each other again.

"Goodbye for now, and may God always protect you!"

The ravens gave a goodbye salute to Elijah.

As they flew up and away, Elijah called out,
"Thanks again for all the delicious food."

Then he winked and added with a shout,
"IT WAS FIT FOR A KING!"

·READ·
1 KINGS 17:1-9

A Whale's Tale

**D**OWN,

DOWN,

DOWN in the deep, dark sea — where sun and moon are never seen, where storm winds never blow, and where water is always so dark and cold and heavy — this is where I like to dive and swim and play.

One day I was playing touch-tag with an octopus and two squid, when I heard God's voice sounding through the ocean, calling me—

"O Great Creature of the Sea, whom I have made with My own hand: Far above you, where the waters touch the air, a ship is being beaten by a wild storm. A man on that ship is trying to get away from Me. At this very moment he's being thrown from his ship into the ocean…"

"That's too bad," I told myself, "But why is God telling this to *me?*"

God's voice sounded again:

"And now, Great Creature of the Sea whom I have made…I want YOU to rescue that man. Now go *up* and swallow him!"

"ME?" I thought. "Swallow a *man?*

YUCK!"

I turned and swam *down* to the bottom of the sea as fast as I could.

133

I KEPT SWIMMING deeper and deeper, to where I'd never been before.
The water got darker, like black ink. I became a little frightened.
The water got colder, like ice. I became *more* frightened.
The water got heavier, like rocks. And I became frantically frightened, because I NEEDED AIR!

"I can't stand it any longer!" I screamed.
"All right, I'll swallow that man!"

So I raced to the top. Everything inside me was pounding:

AIR! AIR! GIVE ME AIR!
AIR! AIR! GIVE ME AIR!

AT THE TOP I let out a blast from my blow-hole, and took in the biggest breath of my life.

Then I saw the man.

"If I swallow him quickly," I told myself, "maybe I won't taste him much."

I gulped him down.

And that was that.

THEN I HEARD MUSIC. Where was it coming from?
I got as still as I could, and listened.
Why, it was the *man* — singing
a *prayer* in *my belly!*

I WAS ALMOST GONE,
ALMOST GONE,
THEN I CRIED OUT TO GOD—
AND HE SAVED ME!

THE STORM WAS DASHING,
THE WAVES WERE CRASHING;
I CRIED OUT TO GOD—
AND HE SAVED ME!
YES, O LORD, YOU SAVED ME!

I THOUGHT I WOULD NEVER
SEE LIGHT AGAIN;
I THOUGHT I WOULD NEVER
BE WARM AGAIN;
I THOUGHT I WOULD NEVER
BREATHE AIR AGAIN;
BUT I CRIED OUT TO GOD—
AND HE SAVED ME!

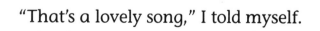

"That's a lovely song," I told myself.

HE KEPT singing
and praying
for three days.

By the second day
I was swishing my tale
in time to the music.

BY THE THIRD DAY
I was singing along.

"I like this," I told myself.
"Maybe I can keep
this music man
inside me forever!"

Then the voice of God sounded
over the ocean—

"O Great Creature of the Sea,
whom I have made:
Take this man to shore!"

"Yes, Lord!" I answered quickly.

I swam for shore, and—
BLLUUUGGGHHHWW! —
I spit up that man
right onto the beach.

THE MAN was standing on the sand. "Thank you for obeying God," he told me, "because you saved me! And now, goodbye. I must go, for God has something for ME to do." The man walked away.

And just as I wondered what God would tell me next, I heard His voice sounding over the ocean:

"O Great Creature of the Sea, whom I have made — return to the deep waters to dive and swim and play!"

"Yes, SIR!" I answered — and down, down, down I went.

READ
THE BOOK OF JONAH

The Night the Lions Played

 HE LARGE, LEAN LIONS were pacing the floor of their den one night — going back and forth, back and forth, back and forth. There was a scowl on each furry face.

As they kept pacing, the biggest lion grumbled and rumbled and mumbled:

"All the day, and all the night —
Tell me, lions, what's our plight?"

"WE'RE STUCK IN THIS HOLE!" the other lions cried out in answer.

146

Back and forth they paced, again and again.
And the biggest lion gnarled and snarled:

"All the day, and all the night —
Tell me, lions, what's our plight?"

"NOBODY EVER FEEDS US!"
they shouted in reply.

Back and forth, back and forth, back and forth they paced.

And the biggest lion growled and howled:

"All the day, and all the night —
Tell me, lions, what's our plight?"

"WE'RE HUNGRY, WE'RE HUNGRY, WE'RE HUNGRY!"
roared the others.

147

JUST THEN, four things happened, one right
after the other, so fast that the lions hardly
had time to think about them.

First, far above them,
the stone was rolled back
from the hole at the top of their den.

Second, a man was thrown down through the hole,
and landed with a *kablump!*

Third, a man with a silver crown on his head
looked down through the hole and cried,
"Daniel! Your God must help you now!"

And fourth, the stone was quickly rolled back over the hole.

The lions circled around the man, and stared at him.

Then they circled a little closer.

And then a little closer.

SUDDENLY an angel of God appeared and stood beside Daniel.

"Go to sleep, lions," the angel said.
"Go to sleep…go to sleep…go to sleep…"

The big lion yawned, and nodded his head, and drooped his eyes.

So did another lion.

And another.

And another.

THEN THE LIONS saw and heard something as fantastic as a dream.

They saw Daniel smiling, and patting their heads.

And they heard him say,
"Why don't we play something?"

All the lions smiled their biggest smiles.

Together, they played Jump-the-Tail.

They played Roll-over, Roll-over.

They played
Stand-on-Your-Mane.

They played
Blind-Lion's-Bluff.

THEN THEY TOOK a break. The lions pushed close to Daniel
so he could scratch their ears.

The biggest lion was so happy and comfortable
he decided to purr like a kitten...

But it came out a loud RURRRR! because lions aren't kittens.
The sound nearly knocked Daniel over.

That was fun too.

THEN THEY ALL decided to play again.

They played
Leap-Lion.

They played
Clap-Your-Paws,
Slap-Your-Paws.

They played
King of the Forest,
and took turns
being King.

And once more they played
Roll-over, Roll-over—
because that was
everyone's favorite.

AFTER THIS they were tired again, and decided to take cat-naps.

As they snuggled up and closed their eyes,
they heard Daniel telling a story about a good man
who always prayed to God.

"Some bad men didn't like him," Daniel said,
"and they passed a law that anyone who prayed to God
should be killed. But this good man kept right on praying.
So the bad men tried to kill him…"

It was a good story, but the lions fell asleep
before they heard the ending.

When they awoke,
they saw Daniel climbing up ropes
and leaving the den.

The lions were sad to see Daniel go. He'd given them such a good time
that they forgot they were hungry.

And they all agreed
it was their Best Night Ever —
the kind of night most lions
only dream about.

READ
DANIEL 6

The Lamb and the
Song of Bethlehem

NDER A STILL AND STARRY SKY, shepherds and their flocks
were settling down for the night on the hillsides near Bethlehem —
the old, old city where the shepherd boy David lived long ago.

Tonight, except for the stars, everything was dark.
The shepherds were singing a song:

Little sheep,
go to sleep;
do not fear,
we are here.
All things new and all things old
now will in your dreams be told;
All things old and all things new,
safe and sound—we're watching you!
Little sheep,
go to sleep;
do not fear,
we are here…

While the shepherds sang, the mother and father sheep
said "Good night" to the lambs at their sides.
"Good night," answered the lambs,
as they snuggled and cuddled and closed their eyes.

By the time the shepherds finished singing, all the sheep were asleep…

All, that is, except one lamb.
Her eyes were wide open, and her head was stretched
as high as her little neck could lift it.
She was watching the sky.

"Mommie!" she whispered. "Mommie!"

160

HER MOTHER stirred awake, and said, "What's wrong?"

"Oh nothing's wrong!" said the lamb. "That music — isn't it beautiful?"

"Music?" said her mother. "But the shepherds aren't singing anymore. You're only dreaming, my darling. You must go back to sleep!"

The lamb was quiet for a moment, but didn't close her eyes. "Mommie!" she whispered again.

"Shhhhh!" her mother whispered back. "Go to sleep, my little one!"

"But Mommie," said the lamb, "I didn't *mean* I hear the music *YET.*"

"*What?*" said her mother.

"I don't hear the music *yet.* I meant it's *coming.* The song is coming!"

"*What* song?" said her mother.

"The *beautiful* song," said the lamb. "The one I just told you about."

The mother shook her head. "I don't understand you, my daughter. If you don't hear any music, how can you say there's a song — and how can you say it's beautiful?"

"Because I *see* it, Mommie," answered the lamb, glancing up. "I see it coming! Look!"

The mother blinked her eyes and looked into the sky. All she saw were stars. But they were brighter — impossibly brighter — than she had ever seen before. "My daughter," she cried, "when did the stars become so bright?"

Her daughter answered, "While the shepherds were singing '*All things old and all things new*'...that's when I saw the stars begin to glow and grow. Mommie, aren't they *beautiful?*"

"They *are* beautiful," said the mother. "Beautiful indeed! But — why do you say there's a *song* coming?"

"Mommie!" exclaimed the lamb. "Why else would the stars get so bright?"

The mother didn't know what to say to that.
She could only stay quiet...and lift her head...and wonder.

Soon she got sleepy again, and forgot all about bright stars
and difficult questions.

AFTER SHE was asleep, her daughter got up
and tiptoed across the field to join the shepherds.

They were standing in silence.
They, too, were staring up at the bright stars.

The lamb saw a shepherd with a friendly face and a curly brown beard.
She rubbed against his leg — and he jumped!

"Ho! Frightened by a lamb!" he said, laughing at himself.
Then he stooped over and picked her up, and laid her across his shoulders.
"Since you're awake," he said,
"you can help us watch this dazzling sky."

SO NOW — a little closer to those flaming stars
than she had been before — the lamb looked up.

And she saw…and heard…and felt…the song
coming nearer and nearer.

SUDDENLY, like silent lightning, a fiery flash fell across the sky.

All around there was light —
holy light — warm light — silent light.
It was as if every star had rushed down to earth,
and without a sound was sweeping through the air
right over their heads.

All the sheep were awake now, and trembling.
One of the shepherds let out a shout.
And all of them fell to the ground.
The little lamb clung tightly to the bearded man's shoulders.

Then — right in the middle of the light —
everyone saw an angel.

The angel spoke, in a voice as bright as the light:

"Don't be afraid!
Behold, I bring you good news of great joy!
For this day — in the city of David —
a Savior is born to you!
He is Christ the Lord!
And this is how you'll see Him:
You'll find the baby all bundled up,
and lying in a manger!"

THEN CAME another flash of light, even brighter.
Suddenly the whole sky was *full* of angels — an army of angels!

They were all praising God — "Hallelu-Yah! Hallelu-Yah!"

And they sang a song — the Beautiful Song:

Glory to God in the highest heaven!
And to all who please God,
let there be peace!

The song rang out,
echoing against the hills,
and resounding in the heart of every shepherd there:

Glory to God in the highest heaven!
And to all who please God,
let there be peace!

Slowly the light began to fade.
One by one the angels started rising up to heaven.
And wherever one of them left the sky,
a star came out to shine again.

Soon, the night was just as it was before —
still… and starry… and quiet.

The curly-bearded shepherd stood up.
"Let's hurry!" he said to the others.
"Let's go see what the angel told us about!"

THEY ALL GOT UP and started running.
In all the excitement, the curly-bearded shepherd
forgot he had the lamb on his shoulders.
So she had a rather bumpy ride.

As they went along, the shepherds sang the Beautiful Song,
for of course no one had forgotten it:

Glory to God in the highest heaven!
And to all who please God,
let there be peace!

WHEN THEY ARRIVED in Bethlehem, they saw exactly what the angel told them they would see. The lamb even got to give the Baby a gentle nudge.

When she came back to the hillside, she found her mother nearly in tears,
and saying, "Where have you been, my precious lamb?
We've been looking all night for you!"

"Oh Mommie!" the lamb answered. "That Beautiful Song —
it was all because of a Baby! I got to see Him, and touch Him!"

And the mother didn't know what to say to that.
She could only stay quiet...and look up...
and wonder.

READ
LUKE 2:8-20

The Prodigal Pig

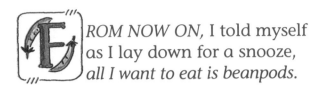

ROM NOW ON, I told myself
as I lay down for a snooze,
all I want to eat is beanpods.

I'd like beanpods for breakfast.
I'd like them for lunch.
I'd like them for a snack in the mid-afternoon.
And I'd like them for supper, so I have a nice full belly
before going to bed.

Yep, I told myself, *to please THIS pig —*
you can't beat beanpods.

We NEVER had beanpods at home.
Just pig-slop.

I told my daddy-pig one day,
"There's nothing good to eat here.
I can't stand it. I'm leaving!"
"Please don't leave us," my daddy-pig said.
"We love you here. We want you here."

"No." I answered. "I'm saying goodbye!"
I slipped through a hole in the fence,
and ran away.

That was yesterday.
Just this morning, I found a new pig-place.

A young man stays here to feed the pigs.
He gives us beanpods.
He fed us piles and piles of them for breakfast,
and I ate most of them myself.
Mmmmmm!

Then I lay down to dream more about beanpods.

The young man sat down on a rock beside me —
which was fine with me,
as long as he kept quiet so I could sleep.

But the young man spoke up:
"Oh, you plump little pig," he said.
"You've filled your belly with beanpods."
I kept my eyes shut, and spoke a little grunt — as if to say,
"Yes, I *have* filled my stomach with beanpods,
and I'd like to dream about them now, if you would please stop talking."

But he continued: "How I long to fill *my* stomach with food!
Even beanpods would be fine," he said.
"But no one gives *me* anything!"

I turned on my other side. — and kept my eyes closed.
I could hear the young man softly crying now.
"What a fool I've been!" he said,
and he let out a sob.

I opened my eyes, and turned back over on my other side.
I couldn't get comfortable. My stomach was starting to hurt.
It felt like it was full of sticks and stones.

The young man was holding his head in his hands.
"I was wrong to run away from home," he cried.
"Everyone in my father's house gets plenty of food.
But here I am *starving!*"

I wished that man would be quiet,
because my stomach-ache was getting worse
and worse and worse.

181

Suddenly the young man stood up, and looked far away.
*I wanted to stand up too, but it hurt too much —
my sore stomach felt like it was full of*

NEEDLES

and

NAILS!

Then the young man shouted,
"I'll go back! That's what I'll do! I'll go back to my father
and I'll say to him, 'Father, I was wrong!
When I ran away from home, I sinned against God
and against you. I'm no longer good enough
to be called your son. But please let me stay with you —
and I'll always do whatever you want me to.'"

"I'm going *home!*" he shouted again.
He ran to the gate, flung it open, and rushed out.

"Ohhh, my poor pig-stomach," I moaned.
It felt like it was full of mud and muck. (Yuck!)

Then I noticed the open gate.
"Why should I stay here?" I asked myself.
"I'm sick of beanpods! I'm going back to my daddy-pig!"

So I dragged myself out.

On the way home, I passed a big house.
Out in front I saw that young man again.

He was getting a big, happy hug from his father.
And his father was saying, "Oh, my son, my son!
You were lost, but now you're found!"

When I finally got to our fence,
I could barely squeeze through the hole.

My daddy-pig was waiting inside.
He squealed with delight to see me, and let out
a hundred happy-pappy oinks — as only a daddy-pig can.

Then we had a big Pig-Slop Party.
And you know...the pig-slop tasted delicious!

The Rich Fish

 I FOUND A COIN one day.
A shiny one.
A big one.

The other fish said to me,
"Just what will you do
with that big, bright coin?"

"I don't know," I said.
"What would *you* do?"

"I'd hold on tightly," said one,
"and never let it go."

"Exactly," said another.
"And I'd swim around the sea,
and show it off."

"Precisely," said another;
"I'd let everybody see
how rich I was."

And they all sang,

> *If we had cash,*
> *we'd let it flash.*
> *We'd make a splash—*
>   *if WE had cash.*

They kept staring at the coin in my mouth,
and their eyes grew bigger and BIGGER and BIGGER.

Slowly, these fish swam closer.

"Let *us* have the coin," they said.
"*We* know just what to do with it!"

"No," I said.
"You're only being greedy!"

"Then we'll *take* it from you!"
they jeered.

I swam away,
as fast as I could.

I swam near the shore.
There I saw a man fishing,
and a little boy coming near him.

"Hello, Simon Peter," said the boy. "Why are you fishing with a pole?
Why don't you take your big net and go out in your boat, like you always do?"

"Because I only want one fish." Peter answered.

"Why just one?" said the boy.

"It's a special fish." he replied. "A fish with a coin in its mouth."

The boy looked back and forth several times from the man to the water. Then he said, "I don't believe there really is a fish down there with a coin in its mouth."

Peter laughed. *"I believe it,"* he said, "because Jesus said so. He wants me to catch that fish — and use the coin to pay His taxes, and mine too."

"Well," said the boy, *"I'll* believe it when I see it."

Suddenly I heard
the other fish closing in behind me.
"Grab that coin!" they said to one another.

So I bit the end of Peter's fishing line.

Peter pulled me up, and gently took the coin from my mouth.

As Peter threw me back in the water,
I heard the boy exclaim, "Jesus was *right!*"
Peter laughed again and said, "Jesus is *always* right."

· READ ·
MATTHEW 17: 24-27

AND DOWN in the sea, the other fish wailed at me: "How foolish of you!" they said. "Now we're poor again!"

But *I* felt richer than ever.

The Bucking Donkey

 E WAS YOUNG — in fact, I still thought of him as my baby. But he was plenty old enough to start learning what donkeys are made for.

"Stop that!" I said to him one day in our stableyard. I didn't like his jumping and kicking all the time.

"But Mother," he said, "I'm just having fun! Besides, I want to be the buckingest donkey there ever was. I'll never let *any* rider stay on me! If he tries to hang on, he'll hit the ground faster than he can say 'Whoa!'"

I blew out a hot breath. "I'll say it once more, my son: God didn't make donkeys to buck people. He made donkeys to *carry* people, gently and carefully—and their packs too."

"Plenty of other donkeys can do that, Mother. I'd rather be a BUCKER!"

"If you're a bucker," I answered gravely, "it will be for a very short time — because men have no need for a donkey that won't be tamed."

"Oh, Mother!" he groaned. He stepped farther away so his jumping and kicking wouldn't bother me. As I watched him, I shuddered to think what might happen if he didn't settle down soon.

Just the day before, I'd overheard our owner talking to his wife. "That new colt is trouble," he had said. "I don't think I can use him; I don't think *anyone* can."

Shaking her head, his wife had replied, "Perhaps we need to get rid of him, one way or another."

NOW AS THE DAY grew hotter, my son stopped his bucking and joined me
in the shade to rest. But when he saw our owner and his wife coming
with ropes to put around us, he jumped up and started kicking again.
After a struggle, the owner got the rope around him.

As he and his wife led us away, the owner said angrily, "Maybe today
we can find someone who needs this unruly beast—because I certainly don't!"

Soon we came to the center of our village. Our owner tied us to a post.
There were people all around, talking and rushing from house to house.
They kept looking down the road to Bethany, a nearby village. "He's coming!"
I heard people saying. "Jesus of Nazareth is on His way to Jerusalem!
He'll be passing through our village today!"

"He's the great prophet!" someone shouted.

"He can raise the dead!" proclaimed another.

"And make food appear from nowhere!" called out another.

Our owner and his wife
got just as excited as the others.

For the moment
they forgot
about us.

I TURNED to my son. "This is probably our last time together," I said with tears. "So listen and be wise! When all this commotion is over, our owner will try to find someone in the crowd to buy you. If anyone tells him, 'I like the way this young donkey looks; let me take a ride, just to try him out' — then do your donkey best to be *gentle, gentle, gentle —*"

"*NO*, Mother!" he protested. "*No one* has ever ridden me, and *no one* ever will. It's no honor to carry a man! I'd rather be wild!"

He stomped the ground, and pulled at his rope.

"Don't you understand?" I cried. "If you stay wild, they'll get rid of you! Won't you please…"

Before I could say more, two men drew near beside us —
two men with kind faces, and who weren't from our village.
They reached for the rope that held my son.

Our owner saw them. "What are you doing?" he called out,
as he and his wife came closer. "Why are you untying that colt?"

The men replied, "The *Lord* needs him —
and He'll send him back shortly."

When our owner and his wife heard that,
their mouths dropped open and their eyes grew wide.
"Of course you may take him, of course," they said.

Then a touch of worry crossed their faces.

Quickly the owner reached forward
and started untying *my* rope.
"In case the little one doesn't do,"
he said with a smile, "take this one too.
She's *very* gentle — yes, a *very* good donkey."

THE MEN LED US away from the village.
Soon we reached a large group of people resting beside the road.
The men took us to the leader of all these travelers.
They called Him Jesus.

When Jesus saw us, He smiled.
He held my son's muzzle in His hands, and gently rubbed him.
It made me wonder if this Man Jesus could someday tame my son.

The people around us were getting up now, ready to start walking again.
"On to Jerusalem!" they shouted.

The men with kind faces took off their cloaks,
and laid them on my son's back. Then Jesus sat down on top.

Jesus didn't seem a bit worried.
He looked as if He rode this young donkey all the time.

I closed my eyes, dreading to hear the awful sound
of my son bucking Jesus off.

But all I heard was people cheering!
I opened my eyes. Jesus was riding lightly down the road —
and my son looked as if he carried Jesus all the time.
I shouted a happy "Hee-haw!" and hurried to catch up with them.
The cheering travelers joined behind us.

With my son and Jesus out in front, our parade made its way
through the crowded streets of the village. On each face I saw a smile,
and from each mouth came a cheer. The biggest smiles and the loudest cheers
were those of our owner and his wife.

OVER A MOUNTAIN we went, and on the other side was Jerusalem.
Even bigger crowds were coming from the city to meet us.
They were waving their cloaks and tree branches,
and laying them on the road for my son and Jesus to pass over.

All the while they shouted praises. The noise was so loud
I almost didn't hear my son shouting too:
"Hee-haw-hosanna in the highest!" he said.
"Blessed is the King who comes in the name of the Lord!"

· READ ·
MATTHEW 21 : 1–11

One Scared Rooster

'M A ROOSTER. But not just any rooster.
I don't live on a farm, like other roosters;
I live in the city.

But not just any city.
I live in Jerusalem, the Holy City;
that's where I do my job.

But not just any job.
The job God gave me is to get His people up and going
every morning. *"Errr-ka-errr-ka-errrrr!"* I crow,
which in rooster language means,
"WAKE UP, GOD'S PEOPLE!
THE DARKNESS IS ENDING,
THE DAYLIGHT IS NEAR!"

I've done my job every day since I was a new rooster—
well, *almost* every day. Let me tell you about the time I *didn't* do it.

IT WAS A HOLIDAY WEEK — the Passover holiday.
Jerusalem was crowded with people who had come to celebrate.

One of those visitors was a Man who stirred up the whole city.

His name was *Jesus.*

ON THE DAY Jesus first rode in, people rushed out to meet Him,
shouting and waving tree branches. The crowd was so big
I almost got trampled — but I wasn't afraid.

The next day Jesus threw some money-changers out of the Temple.
He called them robbers, and turned over their tables.
It was all very loud, but I wasn't frightened.

The next day Jesus made some of the leaders angry, because
He told the truth about the bad things they did.
They looked mean, but they didn't scare me.

Jesus had some friends who stayed close by Him. One of them especially caught
my eye — a man called Peter. He stood straight and tall beside Jesus, proud
to be one of His best friends. Peter looked like a brave man. I liked him.

I SAW Jesus' friends listen to Jesus and obey Him and help Him.
They called Him "Lord." Once, when they were throwing me
kernels of grain, I heard Jesus tell them, "In two days,
some people will put Me on a cross to die."
But His friends didn't seem to believe it.
Peter told Jesus he would never let it happen.
"Yes," I told myself, "That Peter will never be afraid!"

On the last night of the Passover week, the sky was lit by a full moon.
I went strutting through the bright streets to check on my city.
I saw people everywhere staying up late. I pecked at a few toes,
to remind them to get to bed. They needed their rest—
so they could be strong the next day,
and do the jobs God gave them to do.
After all, who knows what tomorrow will bring?

I STEPPED outside the city walls to a garden where olive trees grew. On other moonlit nights I'd often found olives there on the ground — my favorite bedtime snack.

Tonight, under the trees, I found Peter and a few others sleeping.

Then I heard
a strange noise —
but I wasn't afraid.

I turned and saw Jesus
on the ground, yet He
wasn't sleeping. In the
moonlight I saw His
face covered
with sweat.

He was praying.
I heard Him say, "I'm
full of sadness, Father.
And the sadness is so
heavy! But Father,
whatever You want to
happen, let it happen."

I watched Him
for a while. Then I got
sleepy, and I took a nap
right there.

THE SOUND of fast and heavy footsteps woke me up.
Won't this city ever get quiet tonight? I wondered.

A group of men had entered the garden —
some leaders and Temple soldiers. They all had cranky faces,
and the soldiers carried swords and clubs.
Peter at first tried to fight them, but then he slipped off.
The soldiers grabbed Jesus and led Him away.

Jesus needed help! I followed Him back through the gate and into the city.

One of the soldiers tried to kick me out of the way. But he didn't scare me.

We entered a courtyard lit by torches. Lots of people were there—
more soldiers and leaders and servants and others.
They tried to shoo me away, but I wasn't afraid of them.

I wondered where all of Jesus' friends were,
now that He needed their help more than ever.
Were *they* frightened?

I saw Peter sneaking into the courtyard.
I flapped my wings to say hello, but he held his hands in front of his face.
He was acting like he was afraid!

PEOPLE IN THE COURTYARD asked Peter if he had been with Jesus.
But Peter answered, "No!" He said he was absolutely, positively
certain without a doubt that he didn't even know Jesus.

I could hardly believe my ears!
Peter was so afraid *that he didn't tell the truth!*
And he didn't do it just once — I heard him do it *three* times!

After the third time, I decided to crow.
The night was nearly over, and daytime was coming.
In the morning light, I thought, maybe Jesus' friends
would stop being afraid to help him.

I let out my loudest crow: *"Errr-ka-errr-ka-ERRRRR!"*

Then I did it again:
"ERRR-KA-ERRR-KA-ERRRRR!
WAKE UP, GOD'S PEOPLE!
THE DARKNESS IS ENDING,
THE DAYLIGHT IS NEAR!"

I WAS ABOUT to crow a third time, but through the doorway I saw Jesus again. The soldiers were taking Him to another room. As He passed the doorway, Jesus turned His head. For just a moment He looked straight into Peter's face.

Then the soldiers shoved Jesus away.

Peter turned and walked out. I wondered where he would go.

I hopped on the wall, and looked. I saw Peter slumped over in the street, crying harder than I've ever seen a man cry.

Soon the sun came up, and people were awake and out. But no one came to help Jesus.

I followed along as the soldiers and leaders took Jesus to different places in the city. They slapped Him, and beat Him with their fists. They whipped Him, and spit upon Him. And they laughed at Him.

Even the crowds of people who had cheered for Jesus a few days earlier were now screaming that they wanted Him killed.

Yet Jesus didn't scream back. He didn't hit back. He didn't yell at them or tell them to stop.

SOME SOLDIERS made Jesus carry a heavy crossbeam made of wood.

At the top of a hill outside the city, they laid Jesus on the cross.
Then the soldiers nailed Jesus' hands and feet to the wood.

When I tried to get closer,
they threw a hammer at me.

But I wasn't afraid of them.
I'm sticking by Jesus, I told
myself, *no matter what!*

SUDDENLY — in the middle of the day —
the sky got as dark as night.
But there was no moon. There were no stars.

What's this? I wondered. *It's not time to get dark!
Didn't I crow this morning? And whenever I crow,
don't we ALWAYS have a FULL day of daylight?*

Something was terribly wrong, and terribly
scary. My skinny rooster-legs started shaking.

The darkness got darker and darker and darker.

Finally I heard Jesus let out an awful cry...
and then He was silent. I knew He had died.

At that very moment the ground
started shaking — HARD!

I scampered down the hill.
"I'm afraid! I'm afraid!" I squawked.
I found some rocks for a hiding place.
I slumped behind them, and told myself
I would *never ever* come out,
and *never ever* make another sound.
"I'll never crow again!" I said.
"NEVER!"

From my hiding place
I saw daylight come and daylight go.
But I stayed as quiet and still as the rocks.

I was one scared rooster.

I WAS STILL THERE, silent and scared,
when early on the morning of the third day — well before sunup—
a blinding light flashed all around me, brighter than the sun.
I rushed out, ready to run again. But then I saw JESUS coming out of a cave!
He wasn't dead anymore; He was *ALIVE!*

Yes sir, I *saw* Him — and I knew I should never be afraid again.

What a morning!

I fluttered back to the city, and crowed my biggest crow:

"*ERRR-KA-ERRR-KA-ERRRRRRRR!*
WAKE UP, GOD'S PEOPLE!
THE DARKNESS HAS ENDED,
THE DAYLIGHT IS HERE!"

NOW I REALLY have something
to crow about — and I'll never
miss a morning again!

THE BEGINNER'S BIBLE
TIMELESS CHILDREN'S STORIES
(hardbound ★ 528 pages ★ ISBN: 0-945564-31-7)

THIS #1 CHILDREN'S BESTSELLER has more than 500 color illustrations and 95 stories (from Old and New Testaments), all in a durable book that's perfectly sized for little hands and laps.

"It's all here and it's all in order—advanced theology in living color and captivating characters. The stories speak for themselves, but kids will want to hear them over and over again. More than just 'stories,' these words and pictures will become part of your child's life." — **JONI EARECKSON TADA**

"*THE BEGINNER'S BIBLE* is in a class all its own. I've never seen Bible text and illustrations come together with such magical quality. This is the Bible to help every young child vividly experience God's truth. I wish Norma and I had it when our kids were small. We'll certainly make sure it's available to our future grandkids!" — **GARY SMALLEY**

THE BIBLE ANIMAL BAND
SINGING & TELLING THE STORY OF TIME & FOREVER
(hardbound ★ 144 pages ★ ISBN: 0-945564-36-8)

THIS TRAILBLAZING BOOK is an animal's-eye trip through the ages — a look at the grand scheme of things as God designed them, beginning with the dawn of time and flowing on to the future heavenly kingdom that follows time's passing.

Serving as your personal guide on the trip is the one and only **Bible Animal Band**. With each turn of the page these five colorful, talented musicians — **Fargo Fox, Ravey the Raven, Blue Streak the Skunk, Pilla Porcupine**, and **Hogtie the Razorback Hog** — spring to life in illustrations by former Walt Disney animator Jason Lethcoe.

The story they tell is filled with songs and laughter, but has tenderly tragic moments too. From the animal kingdom's unique viewpoint you'll see the terrible fall of man — leading to death on a cross for the greatest Man ever, the one true King of all creation.

It all builds to a heavenly happy ending — and along with the Bible Animal Band you just won't be able to stop singing about it:

> *Never gets old, never gets cold,*
> *more exciting the more it's told,*
> *ever growing, ever longer,*
> *always better, always stronger;*
> *sweet as a kiss,*
> *light as a feather,*
> *a story like this*
> *could go on forever…*
>   *and ever…*
>   *and ever…*
>   *and ever…*
>   *and ever…*